T0195026

Internal Journey of a Writer

The Simple Path to Write Your Novel

Alysia Seymour

BALBOA.PRESS

A DIVISION OF HAY HOUSE

Balboa Press books may be ordered through booksellers or by contacting:

Balboa Press
A Division of Hay House
1663 Liberty Drive
Bloomington, IN 47403
www.balboapress.com
1 (877) 407-4847

Print information available on the last page.

ISBN: 978-1-9822-3838-4 (sc)
ISBN: 978-1-9822-3839-1 (e)

Balboa Press rev. date: 11/11/2019

Contents

Part 1

Floating in the Darkness

MY STORY

Part 2

Breaking Through the Lies

FOUNDATIONS

Part 3

Stepping Into Your Writing Power

PLAN YOUR NOVEL

Part 4

Bringing It All Together to Write Your Novel

Ending Payoff

Rising Into the Light

Dedication

This book is dedicated to those who have supported my writing journey from the beginning. This book would never have been written without your faith in my stories.

Introduction

Before you go any further, know that this book will be unlike any other writing book you've picked up before. I will not give you tools or systems to use, nor will I be providing a definite "how-to" process to create a story, plot, character, or dialogue. This book, is about the internal journey of a writer—the same journey I've been on for the last decade of my life. A journey that is both deeply emotional and highly spiritual.

In this book you will learn how to write your novel. But the journey to get there will look much different than you think. Thinking, in fact, is better left behind while you read this book. Instead, get in touch with what you feel as read the following pages.

I believe there are two paths you can take as a writer.

You can take the path with the most resistance, listening to every Joe and Sally giving you their opinions on what you should do to write a best-seller, or get past writer's block. This will send you into a whirlwind of darkness and despair where nothing you could ever write would be good enough to meet all these expectations, so you never write the book.

Or, you can take the inner journey, the path of spirit and light, trusting that you already have everything you need within to write your book. You thank those who give you their opinion but you let it flow through one ear and out the other, knowing that you don't need any advice or opinion but your own.

This is the simpler path, but it isn't easy. It will ask you to look deep within yourself, to let go of old thoughts and habits that have kept you stuck in your writing up until now. But to be a warrior of light, to step into the role of author, you must seize the sword and claim the title as your own. And this book will show you the way.

So, if you've been spinning your wheels trying to write your novel by following the first path, only to get lost in the cloud of darkness that is fear, doubt, overwhelm and resistance, then I think you'll find this book a refreshing approach, and finally the way to write your book.

This book is designed to take you on the path to finding your faith and confidence as a writer, and to write your first draft, or manuscript. It is not a book that will take you beyond the writing of the first draft—though I will offer some suggestions for what you can do once you've written your draft. The purposes of this book are solely to guide you through the blocks and limitations you set upon yourself that keep you from ever getting started on your novel, and from the cycle of starting but never finishing.

I would like to add is that the second half of this book will guide you through writing a novel. If you want to write non-fiction, then the second half of this book may not be what you're looking for. However, I invite you to rethink writing non-fiction. Read the first half of this book—the foundations (Part 1 and Part 2)—and then decide if you you might not change your mind to tell your story through a fictional lens. Imagination is the place where anything is possible, so why not tell your story through the imagination that fiction stories provide? I've helped others tell their story in this way, and the end results are transformational for them.

If you're ready to take the leap into your own imagination, then let's get started.

Welcome to Internal Journey of a Writer,
Alysia

Part 1

Floating in the Darkness

MY STORY

Discovering Imagination

I could try to be polite about it, or to use a less strong term at least, but the truth is when I worked at the bank, I absolutely hated it. It was an all-day torture of sitting in a cubicle and typing away mindlessly at my computer, completing work for people who could not care less that I existed. They only cared about the numbers. And it showed, certainly so, in the way they treated their employees, and customers alike.

Even if the work environment had been somewhat pleasant, or even top-notch, I would have still been miserable. If you've worked at a job you dislike to any degree, you understand where I'm going with this because when something makes you that unhappy, there's only one simple explanation—it's not right for you.

Yes, others will say that you can make the best of it by changing the way you think about it, and this is true, to an extent, but sometimes—and definitely in my situation— when you feel unaligned with what you're doing, be it a job, a relationship, or anything else, then it's most likely not something you want to spend much more of your time doing.

This was very much the case for me, though I didn't quite see it this way at the time. You see, I'm a dreamer. I've always been a dreamer. Only, I haven't always been aware of this truth about myself, nor confident enough to voice it as a truth. I definitely wasn't in a place to embrace this about myself during this time in my life.

I was about 25 years old, newly engaged, and living my life based on others' expectations of me. I was a people pleaser, especially with my parents and fiancé. I wouldn't do or say anything if I thought they would disapprove or disagree because I just wanted to make them happy. So admitting to them I was a dreamer seemed impossible to me.

Here I am, in the years of my life that are meant to be adventurous and explorative, but I'm stuck at a job I hate, working overtime A LOT, and planning a wedding. In my mind, I needed this job to pay for all of my dreams and fit into the image I thought those in my life had of me.

A year later, I'm married and already pregnant with my first child just a few months into the marriage. Did I mention, I'm still working at the bank and hating every moment that I'm there?

Of course, this affected my relationship with my husband and I fell into a deep depression. I was carrying a child I wasn't ready for, nor did I feel ready to welcome a child. My husband wasn't happy either. I'm sure I wasn't the most pleasant company, so I can't say I blame him.

Why am I telling you all of this, and what does it have to do with writing a novel?

Well, I can say that the one thing that kept me going— even spending hours at a job that made me emotionally and physically unwell, feeling defeated in my marriage, and living up to expectations of other people—was stories.

I listened to books at work and then came home to read

more books. All of them were fiction books because it was my escape from the life I'd very much created for myself, but wanted nothing to do with. Books like *Harry Potter, Lord of the Rings, The Hunger Games, Twilight* (oh yeah, I got into this craze!), *Divergent,* and *A Song of Ice and Fire* are many of the stories that kept me moving forward despite floating within an inner cloud of darkness.

As I said, I'm a dreamer, and a big part of that for me is losing myself in other worlds and characters of fantastic fictional stories. I've been this way since I was a child. And I remember this specific moment where everything changed for me while reading *The Hunger Games.* I was so inspired by Katniss Everdeen and the strength she carried even when she doubted herself. She became a hero to me and I imagined I was her in those difficult moments of my life.

It gave me a sense of strength. But a moment came while as I read the second book in the series, *Catching Fire.*

Why don't I write my own novel?, I asked myself. I love these stories so much it only made logical sense to write my own. Of course, I had no idea what to do, how to do it, or where to start.

And the even bigger challenge, that I didn't understand, which would be a 10-year journey of growth for me—not believing in myself, as an author or as a human being.

Despite having no clue how to write a story like the ones I loved, I began writing. And the more I wrote, the more I dreamed, and before I knew it, I used my down-time at work to write some more. So when the time came that my job fired me for not meeting their expectations—which were made impossible to meet—I celebrated.

I know what you're thinking. Didn't they fire me for writing instead of doing my work? Well, that's not the case because I had two more bank jobs after this one! Yes, you read that right. You'd think I would have learned my lesson after hating my first bank job so much, but oh, I had so much to learn. So no, I wasn't fired for writing on the job. It was one of the other banks after this one I spent my free time writing.

This first bank, was on an agenda to fire people so they didn't have to pay for severance packages during the imminent lay-off. So, I was fired unjustly, and that's okay. I look back now and see everything unfolded as it needed to so I could come to be who I am now, and where I am now.

And even in the daily misery these jobs created for me, they gave me the single, most important thing, which I'm extremely grateful for—my imagination.

But . . . I had a very long journey ahead of me to find my voice, stand up for what I wanted, and step into truth and confidence as an author.

The First Draft:
An Afterthought

I will take some time here, in the beginning of this book, to share my story with you. Not because I love revisiting my life, but because I believe hearing everything I went through to get where I am today—as a confident and successful author—is necessary for you to see it's possible for you too.

I'm also going to insist you read through all of my story and not skip ahead to the next part of the book because you won't get the same value from the practices I will share with you about writing you book unless you understand what must first become in order to begin.

Back to the moment I was fired. I remember that morning so clearly. My supervisor—the one woman in the entire building who cared about her people—came over to my desk. I could tell by the look on her face the time had come, and sure enough she told me I should start getting ready because she would be by soon with the Vice President to walk me out of the building.

I was about to be fired.

The thing is, my supervisor, Ellen, had warned me ahead of time, even before this morning, it was coming.

Like I said, she cared for her people. She also saw a lot of herself in me—the quiet, timid, and antisocial girl—and I think that softened her to me even more than the others.

So the time came. Ellen and the Vice President of the bank walked me out like I was some trouble maker or criminal unworthy of being employed by them anymore. I felt some shame, definitely. I don't know if you've ever been fired unjustly, but it's an awful sensation to know you gave it your best and it still wasn't enough for them.

More the shame though, I felt relief. Relief I would never have to step foot in there again, or face the humiliation of a team of managers who only wanted to weed people out. So there I was, 28 years old being kicked out of a 4-year job, carrying my box of belongings to my car with a mixture of excitement and terror.

To bring this back to writing, let me backtrack about a year from the moment of my firing. Because it was then I decided to start writing my own story, my own novel, while reading *The Hunger Games*, and in that one year I still didn't have a complete first draft written. There were many reasons for this, but the ones we will focus on in this book are overwhelm, self-doubt, and fear.

Yes, I had all three swimming around inside of me like unrelenting piranhas eating away at my insides.

So, when I say I felt both excitement and terror, these emotions not only came from the fact that I had no idea where I'd find another job, earn money, or tell my husband what happened, but they also came from the thought that this could be my moment to make it as an author. I could file for unemployment and spend my time finishing the novel, publishing it, and making enough money to support my family.

Driving away from the bank, a million thoughts coursed

through my mind. Could I do it? Was a worthy enough? Did I have what it took? Would anybody care or support me in this dream to be a published fiction author?

Prior to being fired, I'd spent late nights after I put my daughter to sleep writing my book. Granted, I was so worn out being a new mom and working over forty hours a week, that by the time I sat down to write, I was lucky to get a couple of pages written. But now, I had all the time in the world to write, so that's what I would do!

Wrong.

Instead of spending this time between jobs to get my book written, I spent it worrying about money, or what my husband or parents thought of me for losing a job. To me, it felt if I sat down and wrote my book instead of spending that time looking for another job, I was failing as a wife, mother, daughter, and human being. Then it became this sick inner game of torture where I made myself feel guilty anytime I tried to write.

I was so blind during this time of my life that I couldn't see the truth of what caused me to do this. I thought I was just living like I was supposed to. Working to make a living and taking care of my family. But now, from where I sit, I can see clearly I was floating in the darkness of fear and doubt. These two minions of darkness take on many forms and they're different for each person, but there are some very common threads.

For me fear showed up like this: I wouldn't talk about how I felt with anyone, nor would I confess my true passion in life was to become a successful writer, and I hid behind busy tasks and jobs that didn't serve me just to feel like I mattered or that I was contributing something of worth to the people in my life.

Doubt showed up like this: I didn't believe I had skill

as a writer since I was, after all, learning from scratch all by myself without the means to invest in a mentor or writing program, and my story idea was way too cheesy to interest anyone. They would only laugh at my feeble attempt to become the next J. K. Rowling.

You see, I share my story with you because I believe that it's more common than is talked about to go through these types of experiences. Maybe you're still hiding behind a job you don't like, or staying comfortable in a place that doesn't serve you, whether that's a relationship, a physical location, or something else entirely. And I don't have to guess that fear and doubt are still keeping you floating in the darkness because you've picked up this book.

Don't despair. There is a way out, and I will share with you how I got out of this black cloud in hopes you'll find your way out too. But first, I had a lot more floating to do.

The Journey To
The First Novel

Four months later, and not much more written toward my novel, I had landed my second bank job. It wasn't quite as miserable as my first job ... at least for a little while. Then the true colors of the bank owners started shining through. I worked with the son-in-law of the CEO. He was about 22 years old, if I had to take a guess, and put in charge of me—and only me. He wanted to impress his father-in-law, prove his worthiness of the supervisor title, and marrying into this successful family.

Unfortunately, it came at my expense. He treated me like shit, to be frank. I couldn't do anything perfect enough for him, and every time I did not work up to his expectations, he reported me to the Vice President, whose office sat mere feet from my desk. They wrote me up for things, again, that were out of my control, and when I tried to repeal the write-up, I was called a liar.

It was at this job I started writing at work. I'll admit, I had a very rebellious attitude during these years of my life. I felt like "the man" and these corporate jobs were a joke, and after being treated so unfairly, my instincts proved correct and I just stopped caring. I showed up to work, did what I needed to do—which only took a few hours since work was slow—and spent the rest of my time writing.

Being at my second "real" job and experiencing the same hell as my previous one lit a fire under me. I knew I wouldn't be staying in these jobs for much longer. I knew I was meant for bigger things and that one day, these high-up people would look to me as a world-changer. Okay, I know this sounds arrogant, but I believe all of us who have the deeper calling within us go through this ego-centered moment along our journey to enlightenment.

This was my moment.

I decided to only worry about myself while at work. I walked around with earphones all day so no one would talk to me. I spent the quiet time writing my book, and when a couple of the women in the office noticed, I started talking to them about my book. It was in these casual discussions with co-workers that I started to see a flicker of hope for myself as a writer because these women believed in me and supported my dream. They were impressed I was even tackling writing an entire book! I still had a long way to go, but two things happened to me at this job which were huge steps forward for me as a writer.

I started talking about my dream to become a published author.

I stopped making excuses for why I couldn't write the book.

So I started a routine at this job. I did my work, then I'd sit and write. Sometimes I'd even come home and write more. And this little step forward—talking with a couple of people about what I was doing—plus the fire lit within me at the unfairness of the corporate jobs I felt stuck in, allowed me to finish my book.

It was here, at this small local bank, I did just that.

Now, I'm not in any way condoning that you do the same at your job. Looking back, I can see I was a little hot-headed myself. However, it's the path I needed to take to get my book written, and you will have your own unique nudges to move you forward in your writing journey.

But there is one important fact I want to point out here, and that I want you to understand right now: I wrote my book without seeking a mentor or a program (because I couldn't afford it at the time), and I wrote it purely from my own instincts and intuition I'd built from a lifetime of consuming other fiction stories.

The purpose of this book is to show you you can do the same. After almost a decade of writing novels in this way, I've created a method that allows you to write your book by using all the gifts you have within you. But more on that later.

Back to my first novel . . . I remember the day I finished the draft. I was alone at home and I typed the last words into my manuscript, then I sat there in shock for quite some time (it had been a two-year journey). Finally, I jumped from my chair and shouted, "I did it!". I must have spent about five minutes running around the house in excitement before I collapsed on the ground and just relaxed—half laughing, half sobbing.

My book was done.

But it didn't take long for it to hit me. What now?

I'd written the first draft, did I now have to go back through it all over again for a second draft? That seemed far too overwhelming and terrifying. What if I went back through it and realized how awful it was? Or what if I worked on it, but only made it worse instead of better? Not to mention figuring out the cover design, how to format it, where to publish it . . . it all felt like too much.

And just like that, I fell back into the darkness. Sure, I'd written a *draft* of a novel—few people could say they'd done that. But I still wasn't close to being a published author. Or at least, this is how I saw it. I see everything so differently now—how difficult I made it on myself when it was all so simple.

So again, something that seemed so miserable in my life—meaning this second bank job—had given me something I needed to move forward on my author journey, but still I was far from truly feeling like that successful author I wanted to be.

Stepping Into Authorship

I'd written my first book! I felt proud of myself. But I still didn't voice this dream to many people, especially those closest to me. I thought they would think I was foolish to believe that I could make a living doing what I loved, because it was believed in my family that to make money you had to have a "real" job. And a few more obstacles still waited for me before I would step into my role as an author.

The first, though I don't think of it as an obstacle, was that I became pregnant with my second daughter. This slowed my creativity down a lot—at the time. Now, that I have my new understanding about life and creativity, I wouldn't allow myself to be slowed down quite as much .

Second, the bank where I wrote my book laid me off. They weren't making enough money, and they had to cut back, so everyone except the higher ups were let go. Yep! I'm on a roll. Fired from one bank, laid off from the next. Now I can see though, that this says much more about financial institutions than it does about me as an employee.

Thankfully, I figured out how to finish my book and get it published before either of these obstacles happened.

After finishing, I mentioned I spent some time wallowing over how I would might go through the entire draft again to edit the story. This didn't last too long, and I decided to bunker down and just do it. I found the help of my first supervisor, Ellen—you know, the one from the first bank who saw herself in me. She offered to edit the book for me once I'd gone through it myself. This gave me motivation to keep going.

So I did. The moment I handed the manuscript over to her was nerve-wracking because, until this point, no one else had read the story. And it felt a little ironic to me that someone from the job which made me so miserable would help me get closer to my dream. I guess it embarrassed me. But I still gave it to her. And then I waited . . .

A couple of weeks later, we met for lunch so she could hand me my edited manuscript and share her thoughts. By the end of the meal, I'd sweat through my clothes but I was pleasantly surprised by her feedback. She had plenty of constructive criticism, but overall, she loved the story. I should mention here too that she wasn't a professional editor nor someone who knew the ins and outs of fictional storytelling. I took the help I had available with gratitude, anyway. The bottom line was that she liked the story, and that was enough for me to finish it and get it out into the world!

After this meeting, I went home and spent all the time I could on getting the book ready to publish. I'd also heard about self-publishing through Amazon, which was just becoming prominent. So I now knew how I'd get it out into the world too. Once I got pregnant, I knew I had no time to waste. I was about 4 months pregnant when I published the book on Amazon.

I'll spend a moment here to explain how I got the cover

made, because this isn't the focus of this book, but it is a big part of my journey. My cousin, Tomas Tellez, is a brilliant artist, and he agreed to do the cover for me. He's now my designated book cover artist, and he's done all. Of my book covers. You can check out his amazing work on my website: www.alysiaseymour.com/books

As for editing and formatting, I took what help Ellen had given me and did the rest myself. Some would cringe at publishing a book without first having it professionally edited, but I used what I had at the time—and that was me. I didn't have the money then to pay for an editor (which can be quite an investment), nor did I know where to find a formatter, so I figured it out myself for the digital copies. For print I used some of Amazon's services to create the interior of the book.

Use what you have. Don't worry about what other people believe to be the right way to do something. If you take the time to figure it out, you'll be surprised how much you can do if you're open to guidance from within yourself—your intuition.

I was now a published author—self-published to be exact. My first novel is titled *The Raven Dreams*. I had no idea how to market the book which also isn't the focus of this book, but I felt a huge sense of relief to know that I'd finally accomplished my dream of being a published author.

Yet, something wouldn't allow me to enjoy this experience or to feel that I really *was* an author.

We come back now to that fear and doubt that consumed me when the idea to write the book first entered my mind. Only now it was fear and doubt that I wasn't good enough and no one would read the book. I had a few people tell me they liked the book, but they all knew me personally, so I couldn't allow myself to take those reviews seriously—which is codswallop, by the way. Again, this was my limited view at the time, where now I would take those reviews and make miracles happen!

Since I was preparing for my daughter, I made that my priority and forgot about being an author for quite some time. Two years to be exact. I let my novel float out there in the universe without doing, or saying much about it. My daughter arrived in January 2014. Then in Spring of 2015, I left my husband and moved into an apartment, seeing my girls only half of the time. Many things led up to this but I won't get into them here. But I was very lost, and I blamed my husband for most of it (I see now how wrong I was). I sought things outside of myself for happiness instead of staying true to me, my dream to be an author, and talking to my loved ones about how important this really was to me.

The reason I tell you this is that I spent many dark nights of the soul alone in that apartment and a lot of self-reflection took place. My spiritual journey began. I should mention that I had also gone through two more jobs that sucked the life from me at this point. I'd walked away from my last job, just as I walked away from my marriage to pursue my dream as a writer. This was about a year into my separation, and it was in this moment, free from the constraints of a job, that the idea of writing another book came to me.

I love seeing how I've grown through my novels. As a mentioned, I was on a deeply spiritual journey by this point, trying to figure out what life meant, why I was here, and why I'd gone through so much hell—much of it self-inflicted. This is where the idea for me second novel, *The Wonder Soul*, was born.

Since I'd spent so much time away from writing, it felt a bit foreign at first. But once I started writing, the story just flowed out of me. I'm certain that the difference in writing the second novel was following the spiritual path, rather than an ego-centered path. Ideas, characters and the entire story just came out of me and I poured my heart into those pages, allowing all the pain I'd gone through in recent years to pour out of me. The result was a story about personal struggle, but also about magic and embracing the wonder within us.

I wrote this novel in less than 2 months. Quite a different experience from my first attempt.

Sure, you could say that I had some experience this time. But I know experience had nothing to do with it. It had everything to do with the person I was BEING, versus the person I was when I wrote *The Raven Dreams.*

The book was written, and within the previous year, I'd made great friends with an amazing editor who, when she heard about my book being finished, offered to edit it for free in exchange for using it as a project for her work! Divine guidance was on my side, more proof that my spiritual growth was the key to my success, not any outside experience. So, my book was edited, and in 2018 I published *The Wonder Soul.*

You might notice that this time the editing process took me a bit of time. I'll share with you honestly that I was still living in that fear of not feeling like a real author even though I'd spent years now talking about it and even building an email list of readers.

This time though, my fear was disguised as perfection.

I wasn't aware of it at the time, but I thought I had to make this second novel perfect before I could publish it because it was my second novel, and I would look foolish if I made any mistakes in my *second* novel. I type this with sarcasm because this is completely absurd. But I understand how real it is when you're stuck in that place.

I'd grown a lot as a writer, and as a human being, in this

time. I'd stepped into the role of author. I could feel it inside now. But the growth journey is never done, and while a lot of amazing things were on the way, I still had some challenges to get through to step into my authorship.

Promise Of Transformation

What writing *The Wonder Soul* did for me is magical. It was like my personal medicine to heal old wounds, as well as the fresher wounds of a divorce and feeling like a failed mother. Through the story and characters I learned a lot about myself and taught myself things no one else ever could have. These spiritual teachings, which I believe were sent to me through my writing from a higher power, gave me two amazing things.

I'd grown so deeply—mentally, emotionally, and spiritually—in my time alone and in writing this book, that I could work things out with my husband and bring our family back together.

I discovered I was growing a readership of people, even if only a handful, who truly loved my books.

Yes, my relationship with my ex-husband was restored. But it wasn't just me. He had to be in a place to want to make it work as well. We've now been back together for almost two years. As for the readership, because I had stepped into the role of an author, I was acting more like an author would during pre-publishing days and sending out emails for advanced readers, giving sneak-peeks at my work-in-progress, and just communicating with my email list regularly. So when the time came for reviews, and I received seven 5-star reviews, I began to believe in myself a bit more.

I want to bring this to your awareness, in case it hasn't already arrived in your awareness, because it's very important for the writing journey you're about to begin. The process I used to write my second novel not only gave me confidence as an author, but it also healed me in my personal life in more ways than one.

This shift began to happen for me when I started to have faith in my ability to write a novel, and to stop searching outside of myself for approval, or the "right way to write a book".

And this is the same journey you will take while reading this book. Whether it's your first, or tenth book, whether you've never written a day in your life, or you've tried and failed to finish your draft many times. The internal journey of the writer is a deeply spiritual one, as you'll soon discover.

Back to the publishing of *The Wonder Soul* . . . I was in a good place. I no longer worked at jobs that drained my energy and my sanity. I didn't living separate from my children and I started to *feel* like a successful author on the inside. The problem was, I still dwelt in a place of fear, only this time it wasn't doubt, it wasn't overwhelm, and it wasn't perfection.

It was the fear of not having money.

Despite all I'd accomplished with my books, I still didn't believe I could make a living doing what I love. To mask this fear, I chased after a coaching business I thought would be the answer to this problem. I spent about two years spinning my wheels trying to get this business moving, with very little results. It's not because the business was a bad idea. On the contrary, it was a unique idea with a very heart-centered approach. I wanted to help entrepreneurs write the novel of their life story, to share it in a unique way that wasn't just another autobiography.

It's because I lost track of my purpose that the business didn't pan out. I was chasing someone else's dream of running a successful coaching business because that's what everyone was telling me worked, and forgetting that my dream wasn't that. It was to run a successful author business. To BE a successful author. During this time, I put my writing on the back burner and focused everything on growing this business. The thing is, I was more stressed, unhappy, and sick than I'd ever been.

Looking back, I can see this was because I was out of alignment once again from my true purpose and calling. Yes, I'd reached new spiritual growth on my writing journey, and even some more on my entrepreneurial journey, but I STILL let fear of failure as an author get me off track.

I'd left the corporate jobs behind, but I'd created my own prison trying to build a business I wasn't passionate about in order to make money, because I couldn't possibly make any money from my books. (Notice the sarcasm again here)

It wouldn't be until Spring of 2019 that I would finally see the truth of what I was doing and walk away from that business to focus instead on my novels. Sure, I still didn't make much, if anything from my books for quite some time, but I was feeling better, lighter, and in alignment again. I'm thankful I had the support to make this move because I realize not everyone can just decide to stop making money to pursue their dream.

Regardless of whether you have support is irrelevant.

What matters is that you know what your purpose and calling are, and move toward them every single day. Sometimes that might look like putting in the work toward your novel, other days it might look like taking the day off to rest or enjoy something just for fun. This concept took me a long time to practice. I'd lived my life believing I wasn't contributing anything useful unless I was working to bring in money. When I stop and think about that mindset now, I realize how ludicrous it was to ever hold that belief. Yet, I know most of us do hold the same belief.

Yes, you need to pay rent, buy food, and provide other basic needs for you and your family. But how much money you make, whether it's $0 or $1,000,000, does NOT define your worth. It's easy to forget this when you're on your purpose path and the struggle sets in. But struggle is also just an illusion that we choose to believe. It doesn't have to be a struggle. It can be simple.

My point is, my last challenge was to overcome this belief about needing to make money with my work in order to matter. To this day, I still have to remind myself of this truth, regardless of how much money I'm making. It was a deep-rooted lie that I chose to believe at some point in my life, and looking back at my struggle with jobs, I can see how deep and far back it really went.

What happened when I left this business behind and returned to my truth as an author? I wrote and published my third novel, *The Raven Wars*, in a three-month period. I stopped playing around, stopped dabbling in the writing, and took it on as a serious, I-want-to-be-this, endeavor. *The Raven Wars* is Book II in *The Raven Dreams Series*. That's right, I made it a series! And after I write this book that you're reading now, I will write Book III.

The books are just flowing out of me now. Did I mention

that once I complete this series, I'm already planning a middle grade series, and after that an entirely new young adult series? This is who I am now, and I no longer doubt myself, my writing, or the money. It took me almost a decade, but I finally stepped into my role as an author, for real. The passion I have inside for storytelling is unlike anything else I've ever felt, and I don't worry whether people will like my books anymore. I know the right people will love them, and those who don't aren't my readers.

It was a long, sometimes cruel, journey to reach this place but I wouldn't change any of it, because without those struggles I wouldn't be where I am now. And here's the good news for you . . . because I've already gone through the struggle, and figured out how to break free from it, I will show you how you can do the same thing, but in much less time and with much less struggle.

I only warn you of this: you're about to embark on a deeply emotional and spiritual journey, and it will require you to grow your faith in yourself and a higher power to write your book.

I mentioned in the beginning pages of this book that this will be unlike any writing book you've read before. It's about to take a turn and get really good. If you agree to this, and you're ready, turn the page.

Part 2

Breaking Through
the Lies

FOUNDATIONS

External Writer's Journey Vs. Internal Writer's Journey

Now that I've shared my writer's journey with you, it's time to shift into how you can apply this journey for yourself. As I said, I didn't share my story for kicks and giggles, but to show you how I came to the understanding that searching for the answers of "how-to" write my novels outside of myself wasn't the way to go. I hope you saw how I shifted over those eight years from a place of fear and doubt—not only in myself but in a higher power—to a place of peace and confidence as a writer and human being. Writing stories now is not only simple, but it's empowering and extremely fun.

I want to take some time now to look at the two different ways your can approach your writing journey.

I like to call them the *internal writer's journey* and the *external writer's journey*. At the beginning of my story in this book, I was very much operating externally, and not just in my writing, but in everything in my life. I had no sense of self, nor how to bring my dreams to be. That showed in my continuous search for jobs that didn't serve me just to earn a paycheck and in the struggles I faced trying to write my first novel. When you operate in this way, creating your external world as the all-encompassing reality and believing that nothing magical can happen, you shut off any possibilities of the truth reaching you.

The truth is that *everything* is possible if you accept it as so and have faith that it's on its way to you.

I will come back to this statement in a moment, but first, I want to talk in detail about the *external writer's journey* because I know this is where most writers, and humans, live from—the external journey, or external world. What does it look like? Let me break it down for you by detailing what a writing day looked like for me when I first began the writer's journey in 2011.

I wake up, tired and unmotivated, cursing my alarm for going off too early. I mean, can't I just sleep the day away? That would be much easier than facing all these things I don't want to do, or be. Crawling out of bed, I forced myself into the shower, get ready for work, and down a cup of coffee before rushing to wake my daughter to take her to my parent's house. There are fits, yelling, and sometimes tears—and I'm not talking about my one-year-old daughter here, I was just as prone to all of it as she was.

By the time I'm driving to work, I'm frazzled and stressed out. Traffic brings down my mood even further so that by the time I arrive at work, I'm already in a miserable state of mind, only to be made more miserable by sitting 8 or 9 hours at a job I don't want to be at. I leave the job to drive in more traffic, pick up my daughter, come home to a messy house and cook dinner, get her ready for sleep and finally stumble to my computer around 8 o'clock at night to write a few paragraphs or pages. By this time, I'm in no mental state to be creative and it feels forced, even unwelcome, to get the story out. I fall asleep at the desk and finally give up to crawl into bed, dreading the next day.

Sounds awful, doesn't it?

Yet this is the truth for more people, than not. And if you're a writer, or you aspire to be a writer, this won't cut it. You simply cannot write the story you're meant to, that's part of your purpose in this lifetime, if you're constantly miserable and drained.

Here's the other aspect of taking the *external writer's journey*, and trust me, I know it well since I lived it for several years. When everything outside of yourself determines your worth and your success, you will by default search despairingly for other people to tell what to do—should you write fiction or non-fiction, how do you tell a compelling story, what makes a good character, how do you create a plot, what does every successful novel have that makes it so . . . and on, and on it goes. Google becomes your best friend, and at first this seems like a fantastic idea.

Don't get me wrong, Google is fantastic to search for the right reasons. But when you're beginning, and you're in a place of fear and doubt, it will only push you further down a hole until you feel hopeless and overwhelmed. So you keep searching, reading all kinds of articles, blogs, program descriptions that make all these promises such as, if you complete these five steps or include these ten rules in your story, then you'll be successful. But you can't see it as true for you because you don't yet have the faith or the confidence in yourself, or your writing, to believe it.

In some instances, these articles and blogs are bullshit,

anyway. People who want to earn a quick buck selling tips online. Others are amazing offers, and can take your writing to new levels, but you have to BE in the place where you're ready to hear what they're saying and apply it. The truth is, when you're starting out, or if you've tried and failed before, you're not there yet. You first have to find the belief within yourself, and no one can give that to you, except for you.

The last aspect to consider when looking at taking the *external writer's journey* is writing groups. I've never been part of a writer's group. The closest I got to one was an online group that met once a month, but we didn't talk too much about our writing, and more about our lives. I think these groups can be fantastic for some people, but they aren't for everyone. I especially wouldn't recommend you join a writing group if you're still stuck in that place of fear and doubt, because it will only take you further down the hole just like Google. While those groups usually have the best intentions at heart, the opinions of others—and opinions that may not be valid at that—can wear on your confidence and overload you with unnecessary information. I will keep saying this: you *do not* want that.

To become confident and successful as an author, you must feel it inside of you without the opinions and advice of others. In fact, it doesn't matter in the slightest what other people think about "how" you're writing your book or novel. The only thing that matters is that it works for YOU.

So, when you're operating from this external place, meaning you're giving everything and everyone outside of yourself the power to tell you what to do, when to do it, and how to do it, you simply won't step into that role as an author.

Before we move into what the *internal writer's journey* looks like, let's take a look at a very well-known and

successful author who is living proof of this truth, to ignore the outer circumstances altogether.

Stephen King. If there ever was a prolific fiction author who changed the way the world viewed fictional stories, he is definitely a big one. In his book, *On Writing*, he shares his own very personal journey as a writer that involved all kinds of struggles and road blocks, like drugs and his marriage nearly falling apart. In this book, he has much wise advice for writers at every level, but these specific quotes stood out to me, and apply to what we're talking about:

> *For any writer, but for the beginner writer in particular, it is wise to eliminate every possible distraction. (Pg. 156, Stephen King, On Writing)*
>
> *What are you going to write about? And the equally big answer: Anything you damn well want. Anything at all . . . as long as you tell the truth. (Pg. 158, Stephen King, On Writing)*
>
> *What would be very wrong, I think, is to turn away from what you know and like in favor of things you believe will impress your friends, relatives, and writing-circle colleagues . . . or in order to make money. (Pg. 159, Stephen King, On Writing)*
>
> *I distrust plot for two reasons: first, because our lives are largely plotless, even when you add in all our reasonable precautions and careful planning; and second, because I believe plotting and the spontaneity of real creation aren't compatible. (Pg. 163, Stephen King, On Writing)*

Let's take a look at each one individually:

For any writer, but for the beginner writer in particular, it is wise to eliminate every possible distraction. I believe what he's referring to here is twofold. First, when you sit down to write make sure that any distractions have been removed from your writing space. No cell phone (or put it on airplane mode/do not disturb), no browsing the internet, unless for specific book research (I like to separate my research time from my writing time), no television or loud conversations happening around you, and anything else you can think of. It's just you and the keyboard creating the story together. Second, every possible distraction outside of yourself such as opinions of others, even influencers, as well as ignoring that little voice in your head that's telling you all the reasons you can't, or you're not good enough, or the story isn't good enough.

What are you going to write about? And the equally big answer: Anything you damn well want. Anything at all . . . as long as you tell the truth. Here he's addressing that all-too-popular question, which is really fear and doubt in disguise—What story should you write? I love Stephen King's perspective on this because it took me a long time to have confidence in my first novel and the story I chose to tell. For me, it was never a question that I would write about what I wanted to, but it was the fear that what I wanted to write was a joke. But the important message he's giving us here is that you can write about absolutely ANYTHING you want to, just tell the truth. That means writing what you *know*, and only what you know, so you know it's truth. It also means writing what you feel on the inside. The truth of what you feel, not some paled-down version of it. If you worry about offending people, you'll never write the book or novel that will change lives.

What would be very wrong, I think, is to turn away from what you know and like in favor of things you believe will impress your friends, relatives, and writing-circle colleagues . . . or in order to make money. Again, stick to what you know—what you enjoy and what lights you up. It's here, in this place that you will find the most confidence in your story, and as a writer. If you try to write a book by first looking out into the world to see what's big right now, or which authors are on the best-seller list so you can mimic their work, you will always lose and always feel empty inside, even if you finish the book. And even if it does do well, it won't feel like your story, so you won't enjoy the success like you otherwise would. The last bit about money . . . oh boy. Don't get me started. Many aspiring authors think they will write that book and become an immediate success, and yes that can happen, but it doesn't always. If you're only writing this book in hopes you'll make big bucks from it, stop writing now. You must find within you the passion to write because it's what lights you up and because that story within you must be told.

I distrust plot for two reasons: first, because our lives are largely plotless, even when you add in all our reasonable precautions and careful planning; and second, because I believe plotting and the spontaneity of real creation aren't compatible. This one comes back to the idea of not taking every single opinion out there seriously and trying to apply all of it to your own book. One of the big questions fiction authors ask is to outline, or not to outline; to map it out, or take it from the seat of your pants? While Stephen King is clearly siding with to "no outline" group, I also believe that here he's speaking in terms of knowing what works for you and what doesn't. If you feel great about outlining, by all means do it. But if you're only doing it because some more advanced writing guru said you have to, DO NOT. Life is an ebb and flow, as is writing. Let it flow from you as it will.

Now that you have a clear understanding of what the *external writer's journey* looks like, let's take a look at the *internal writer's journey*.

I'll start by sharing the contrast of what my days look like now, in 2019, as I write this book compared to how they looked when I walked the *external writer's journey* all those years ago. I wake up in the morning with excitement and a sense of peace. Sometimes I'm still tired, but that's because I have very intense dreams that won't let my mind rest at night (that's an entirely different book), yet the tiredness wears off quickly as I move into my day. I shower and go straight to my morning meditation. Then I have a cup of hot water with lemon and read for ten minutes. By this time, I have to pack lunches and wake my daughters to get ready. I drop them off at school, listening to one of many inspirational podcasts I follow on the drive back, and come home to exercise. Sometimes I do yoga, sometimes a workout video, and sometimes, both! Once I've had breakfast, I sit down to write between 9am-10am and stay there for a couple of hours. The words flow so easily and I feel pumped up after each writing session. I'll break for lunch, go outside for a bit and come in to write a little more. I'm usually done by 2pm, so I have some wind down time before I pick my kids up from school. We spend a good evening together with dinner, homework and family time.

I look forward to the next day when I can write more and spend time with my kids, always feeling a sense of deep peace as I do all of it. Can you see the difference here? Living externally caused so much anxiety, fear, and depression, while living internally created peace and inspiration, not just for my writing, but for my life.

I like using Stephen King's quote's in between the *external writer's journey* and the *internal writer's journey* because I feel he gives really good insight on how to make the shift from one to the other. I'll talk more about this shift in the next section. But first, more on what the internal writer's journey looks like.

While I can't speak for every writer, I can tell you how I found this inner journey and embraced it. Let's explore this by contrasting the inner journey with each point I referenced in the external journey. So, for example, searching Google endlessly for answers on "how-to" write your book or novel. I used to be a master at this one, but now I will not visit Google for anything except to look up the meaning of a word, or to find a synonym, or to research a subject I need more knowledge on to write the story.

Even when I wrote my first novel, I quickly stopped using Google because I realized that the information overload made my head spin and I became less productive. Instead, what I do is get quiet, say a short prayer or intention before my writing session, and let the story flow. It amazes me how much I can write in a short time when I use this approach to writing.

This is true for any stage of the journey: creating the book idea, outlining if you choose to do so, creating characters, deciding on a genre, and all the rest.

Writing groups follow the same direction in my life— meaning they have no direction because they don't exist for me. I don't use writing groups of any kind, nor do I intend to. I see the time I would spend talking with a group of people as time I could otherwise spend writing the book. And since my writing time is limited as it is, being a work-from-home mom, I treat my writing time with precious protection. If you are in a group, and you find value there, by all means keep going. DO NOT go because you think you have to, or because you think someone there will have all of your answers.

The *internal writer's journey* is really as simple as this: get quiet, meditate, hold an intention for the ideas to flow through you, then sit and write.

This may be a tough concept for many people to grasp right now. If you've lived an externally focused life, it probably sounds completely ludicrous. But I promise you, it's not. I mentioned at the start of this section that *everything* is possible if you accept it as so, and have faith that it's on its way to you. And in the section that follows, we'll get deeper into how you can make this shift and grow faith in yourself and the writing process in order to write your book and get it out into the world.

Moving From Your Head Into Your Mind

When you're working from your head, you see everything as cause and effect. If you work X amount of hours, then you'll earn X amount of dollars. If you "keep your body in shape" and "wear the right clothes", then you'll attract the perfect partner. Things appear to you as limited in option, and you cannot see beyond the processes of your thinking mind.

When you're living from your heart, you see everything as energy. Your body, money, relationships, material possessions, all of it. It's all energy. Here, things appear as unlimited. Everything is created from this same energy, therefore we're connected to everything, including our book that hasn't been written, and the money we desire.

Another way to view this shift instead of your head versus your heart, is shifting from your head to your _mind_.

Let's look at quote from someone who changed the world in miraculous ways:

"Be willing to dream, and imagine yourself becoming all you wish to be. If you live from those imaginings, the universe will align with you in bringing all you wish for—and even more than you imagined . . ." —Wayne Dyer, Wishes Fulfilled

When we talk about the head in this book, we're referring to all the aspects I mentioned in the first lines of this section: everything is cause and effect. In other words, your ego is running the show. The ego will send you all kinds of lies to keep you in a place of worry, fear and doubt. You're operating from a limited point of view, one that exists only in the physical world.

Your mind, on the other hand, is synonymous with your heart because they're connected. Your mind, when driven by your heart, operates from a place of imagination and faith. Here, you're connecting the the spiritual world where anything is possible. You believe, not only in yourself, but in a higher force, the Universal Power, that's giving you everything you ask for—good or bad.

The problem is, we are usually asking for things we don't want without being aware we're doing it. It's at a subconscious level. We wonder why we can't write the book or create the success we want, but we fail to look within ourselves, to our minds—or our thoughts—to see how we've created all of these circumstances for ourselves purely from our own imagination, or thoughts.

Our minds our so powerful, anything we ask for and believe in with conviction, will come to pass in our physical world. The secret is to become aware of the thoughts you're having and replace them with thoughts, or imaginings, of all you want to create. Instead of having all the fearful thoughts about not being good enough to be a writer, not believing anyone will like your story, or thinking you will be judged for your book, change your thinking! Tell yourself,

"I am a brilliant writer", "I am finishing this book", "I am in possession of all I need to write this book".

Wayne Dyer was exactly right. Using your head causes you to operate only from the knowledge you have. While using your mind—in the right way—allows you to imagine all you desire and that will give you all you ever wanted. The Universe aligns with your thoughts, which exist in your mind, so make them empowering thoughts of the writer that you are RIGHT NOW. Because you already are that writer who has success and confidence, you only need to step into the role and believe it as truth now.

Coming back to the *internal writer's journey*, using your imagination along this inner journey is key. But to use your imagination in a way that serves your dreams as a writer, rather than hinders them, you must be able to quiet your mind of all the excess chatter that goes on in your mind throughout the day. Because the majority of that chatter is negative: worrying, denying yourself, fearing judgment, talking yourself out of things, and more. You want a clear space where you can be free to imagine all you want without simultaneously telling yourself it's impossible.

This is why getting quiet, meditating, holding the intention for the ideas to flow through you, then sitting down to write is the path to the *internal writer's journey*. Let's take a look at each of these individually:

Get Quiet

Meaning, get to the quiet place in your mind where your thoughts slow down, and more and more of them are serving your highest good. Stop letting the chatter rule you. Become conscious of the thoughts you're thinking. You get to *choose* what thoughts you have. Only, you need to step into the role of Thinker rather than being a victim to your thoughts. YOU are the Creator, the Thinker, and only you control which thoughts you give attention to. If the mind chatter doesn't stop right away, just choose to ignore all the unwanted thoughts, letting them pass by like a cloud, and instead focus on the thoughts that will create what you want. Like success as an author, or holding that completed manuscript in your hands.

The more you can ignore unwanted thoughts, or eliminate them altogether, the quieter your mind becomes. And when your mind is quiet, those ideas and creative juices for your book can flow freely to you. It will feel like something is working through you to translate the words onto the page. And it is—a higher power, your highest self, is showing you the way as soon as you step aside and quiet your mind to let it shine through.

Meditation

The world we live in today makes it very difficult to keep our minds quiet, or so it seems. We have all this technology, media, and quick solutions to what seems like every problem, yet inside of ourselves, we're spinning out of control, unable to keep our physical or mental self still. The easiest, and in my opinion, the only way we can quiet our minds is through meditation. Meditation is the place where we open ourselves to receiving what the Universe wants to send us—what we truly desire. The trick is you don't ask for what you desire, but instead get quiet and connect to the inner place of peace and love within. Just sit in silence meditating on nothing but the void, the space in-between your thoughts.

This might seem impossible at first, but each time you will find yourself getting deeper into that space where you can create miracles. And in our case in this book, that miracle is writing your book. There are many amazing meditations available out there for nor charge. I'm a fan of Wayne Dyer's *I Am Wishes Fulfilled Meditation* and *Meditations for Manifesting.* They have truly transformed my inner world to one that allows me to open myself to creativity and imagination. Writer's block, fear, doubt, overwhelm—all of those have left me so I can write from peace, where the ideas flow to me with ease. Another good meditation resource is a free app called, *Insight Timer.*

Give it a try. I know it can sound like hocuspocus at first, but once you actually experience it, you will see meditation for the magic it truly is.

Hold the Intention

If you listen to either of the meditations above, you will find more guidance on the power of I Am statements, but it's basically holding the intention that you want to create in your imagination, until it arrives. *I am writing with ease every day, I am finishing my manuscript, I am writing with confidence, I am inspiring thousands of readers with my book.* Or you can say "I intend . . ." and then fill in the blank for what you want to create. Using your imagination is all you're doing here. Picture your intention in your mind, feel it in your body, as if it's here right now, because it is!

You've only stepped in the way of it coming to you through negative thinking. Step out of the way through quieting your mind in meditation and just hold that intention. Your completed book is already here, you just have to believe it and it will be written through you from that higher self.

Write

While it all seems quite magical, and it is, you also must take the steps to creation. The book will never get written if you never sit down at the keyboard and type the words. But I can promise you, once you get into that quiet space more frequently, you'll find yourself more eager to write the book. Ideas will come to you when you least expect, and it will light that fire in your very being urging you to go write. Other days, you may need to drag yourself to the computer, and that's okay too. Even if you don't write some days, that's okay! Because you will come back tomorrow, or as soon as the next nudge urges you along. Trust in the process—both spiritual and writing. Let the Universe guide you.

Practice these every day, for as much of the day as possible. Yes, you most likely will not sit in meditation all day, unless you want to! But become aware of your thoughts, and one-by-one remove the ones that no longer serve you in your dream to write a book, instead focusing on all the intentions you're holding for your good. Before you know it, you'll be writing your book and sending it out into the world.

I hope you're beginning to feel the shift from your head into your heart, or rather from your head into your mind. And now you can begin guiding your mind, using it to thrive rather than create more struggle. Keep this idea close with you as we move into the next section on excuses, and know that all excuses come from your ego, or the fear that lives in those chattering thoughts.

Letting Go
Of Excuses

If there's one thing that will stop you on your path to becoming an author, it's excuses. What I've found along my writing journey, talking with other writers and aspiring writers, as well as my clients is this: your book is the first thing to be placed on the back burner when life gets too hard, or busy, or you get sick. It never fails.

You intend to wake up early to write before you leave for work, but during the night your child wakes from a bad dream and keeps you up, so you're too tired to get up that little bit earlier you were planning on.

After work seems like the perfect time to sit down and write in some quiet, but then work ends up being stressful and after eating dinner you feel tired, so instead of writing you binge-watch some Netflix shows.

This one is my favorite: You actually *do* sit down to write, but then something you call "writer's block" prevents you from getting any words onto the paper and you give up, deciding it's not meant to be today.

These are some examples, both from my own life, and that I've heard from others who *intend* to write their book, but never do. And these are all the same thing—excuses. It might seem like it's out of your control, something outside of yourself preventing you from writing—for example, your child waking you up at night and keeping you up for a while—but it really comes down to your own faith and conviction of whether or not writing this book is a priority for you.

If it is, you'll still get up early when the alarm goes off . . . maybe have an extra cup of coffee and get writing. Or you decide that you'll sleep until your normal time, but you'll stay up a bit later that night to write. They key is that you **do it**. If you do, you've made your book a priority. If it's not a priority for you, you'll wake up at the same time, cursing life, or maybe even your child, for impeding your creativity and you give up on trying for a while.

I did this A LOT at the beginning of my writing journey, so I say this from personal experience, not as judgment. But the simple truth is, all of this negative self-talk about why you can't write your book is nothing more than excuses. Here are a few more really common excuses:

> *There's not enough time.*
> *I'll do it tomorrow.*
> *I have to wait until I have the perfect idea, or until I know exactly what I'm doing.*
> *People won't like this book anyway, so there's no point in trying.*
> *I'm too tired/sick/busy.*

All excuses.

Let's pause here to take a look at what excuses really are. If you've been paying attention, you'll already know

the answer to this. I mentioned it at the end of the last section. Excuses are nothing more than FEAR in disguise.

That's it. It's easier said than done to shift your perspective to seeing your excuses as fear, let alone shed yourself from this fear in order to move forward with your book—or so it seems to the logical thinking mind who only operates from limited knowledge. BUT . . . if you shift into your mind, where your imagination is free to create as it pleases, nothing can stop you from stopping the excuses and letting go of the fear.

So how are these excuses fear, exactly? Take the example of the parent who's lost sleep because their child woke up in the night. The ego will tell you it's out of your control and that writing isn't meant to be today. It will make you believe in a flash of knowledge that rises in you from thoughts such as: *I'm too tired to write now;* or, *Life isn't working for me today, what's the point?* The fear is hidden from your logical thoughts, or mind chatter, but it's there.

Fear is hiding in the moment you decide to give up.

As soon as you give up on your dream to write, allowing external circumstances to determine your fate, you've let your fear take over. It could be fear of being unworthy, fear of the world working against you, or simply a fear of being too tired at work if you were to still wake up early. It's the same for all the other excuses I mentioned above. Whether it's a belief in lack of time or confidence, that you're too tired or sick, it doesn't matter. Hidden within all of those excuses is a fear of being seen, being judged, being laughed at, of failing, of not being good enough, and on, and on.

When you allow the external world determine your path, you will always lose. As soon as you react to a situation that prevents you from writing with negative thinking, you've handed over your power to that circumstance and the book never gets written, or it gets postponed a great deal.

This brings us back to living the *internal writer's journey* rather than the *external writer's journey*. When you quiet your mind, meditate and hold intentions for your completed book on a daily or regular basis, these types of reactions and excuses become less prominent in your reality. They naturally fall away from your life. You may even find that circumstances stop interfering with your writing at all. You become less reactive to what's happening on the outside and stay connected to that calling that's within you to write your book. When you're connected to that calling at a deep level, nothing will stop you from getting it written.

The way to stay connected, or to reconnect, to your calling is by living the *internal writer's journey*. The excuses will slowly decrease until they no longer show up, and your life will magically open up pathways and moments for you to sit and write. All of these excuses boil down to two major enemies which all writers must face, at least in the beginning. And yes, these are also fear in disguise. But like all other excuses, you can remove them from your reality by going within using everything we've talked about so far.

Two Worst
Enemies Of
Writers

As I mentioned, these two enemies—as we're calling them for imagination purposes—are the cause of *all* your excuses, and masked as fear. The first we will talk about is *overwhelm*. This is very similar to what I talked about when I outlined the *external writer's journey* to you a few sections back. Overwhelm comes about when you're so focused on everything outside of yourself—such as, only writing a book because it's a popular idea, or constantly searching for others' opinions on how you should be writing—that you spin your wheels, overthink, make yourself, sick, and any other prevention that will keep you from writing your novel.

It looks like: hoarding dozens of books on "how to write", every other opinion on Google searches stress you out, asking friends and family if they think your idea is good enough for a book, flip-flopping back and forth over whether you'll write the book or not.

This can go on for weeks, months, or years. The longer

it lasts, the worse it feels, until you decide writing a book isn't worth all of this turmoil and you stuff the book away— in your mind, or on your computer. or in your desk. It's forgotten about for a time, but it never really goes away . . . this calling. Then you beat yourself up for not writing it, playing the guilt game until you're stressed out and unhappy, you finally decide you can't live with yourself and you bring the book out only to go through the same cycle all over gain.

It's miserable. Yet, this is what so many beginner writer's go through. I went through it, though thankfully not for too long. And I'm here to break that cycle for you right now, if you are stuck there. But first, let's talk about the other enemy, then I'll share with you how I got passed them.

The second enemy is much more internal, and it's *self-doubt*. Unlike overwhelm, which comes from external factors, self-doubt is a deep-rooted, internal battle with yourself. Outside experiences can influence your level of self-doubt, but the truth is that it starts from within you, based on beliefs you hold about yourself. Self-doubt is summed up by thoughts like: *I'm not good enough, Who am I to be a writer, No one will like my book, etc.*

If you're prone to this type of thinking, it's no wonder that self-doubt will prevent you from ever writing your novel. You may have a wonderful idea to write about, but you just don't believe in yourself and those thoughts keep circling in your head, making you believe less in yourself. And, just like with overwhelm, you stuff your story away because you can't even bring yourself to *try* to write. It's a different place to be, whereas with overwhelm many will at least try to write the book, though with misguided intentions.

When you live in self-doubt, even thinking about trying to sit down and write sends fear pouring down your back like a cold bucket of water. It's enough to send you running to hide in a corner or under the covers of your bed until the foolish idea that you could one day be a published author leaves your mind.

If it's possible, this is even more miserable a place to be than operating from overwhelm. But the bottom line is that both overwhelm and self-doubt eat away at your creativity and you once again have become so focused on fear brought on by negative thoughts that you're living the *external writer's journey*. I intend by now that you're getting a clear picture of the difference of the internal and external journey and you're beginning to see how freeing the *internal writer's journey* is.

So what is the answer to freeing yourself from overwhelm and self-doubt? It's really quite simple, but far from easy . . . at least in the beginning.

The answer is: start writing.

Please don't throw your book across the room, or yell into the pages hoping that I'll hear your curses from whatever distance apart we may be. Hear me out.

I'll be honest, if someone had told me this as the answer to my writing problems at the beginning of my writing journey, I would have rolled my eyes at them and walked away mumbling four-letter words under my breath. So, actually, if you need to yell or throw your book in this moment, go ahead. Just don't break your eReader in the process!

This is it, what we've been working up to. Afterall, this book's subtitle promised to give you a solution to write your novel. It was inevitable that we would arrive at the moment that you'd actually have to start writing, and here it is. The answer to remove overwhelm, self-doubt, and any other excuse or fear is to start writing your book. But remember all you've read up until this point, because it's key.

Write from within, not from searching outside of

yourself for any idea or story guidance. Use imagination rather than knowledge to write your book, and nothing else. Quiet your mind through meditation and intentions.

When you can write your book from this place, rather than from an external place where opinions and fear rule you, sitting down to write becomes much less intimidating. I will guide you through the process of doing this in the pages that follow. It's the way I write my novels, and how I've helped clients to write their novels as well.

I would even suggest that if you're considering writing non-fiction, to rethink that idea and instead write a novel that tells the story you want to tell. Leave non-fiction behind and really dive into your imagination to share from your heart, heal your wounds, and inspire others by allowing them into the more personal story you have to share, rather than writing it in non-fiction format. Every one of my novels is my life turned into fiction. This is the journey we are taking now.

They internal writer's journey we're about to begin is one that's connected to your emotions and your spirit. Everything you need will come from within you.

Again, I will guide you through this process. You're about to embark on a magical and life-changing experience where you will not only write your book, but you will step into who you really are and change your life. Stay open and get ready to be vulnerable. No one has to see what you've written until you're ready.

Part 3

Stepping Into Your Writing Power

PLAN YOUR NOVEL

Discover
Your Story

We spent the first half of this book setting the foundation for the writer you want to be to create your dreams of being a published author. It's a shift from living an outwardly focused life, to being focused only on your own inner world. It's from this place where imagination and magic take over and the stars align for you to write your book. And not just any book, but the most impactful and inspiring book you could write. Now it's time to shift from concepts to inspired action. It's time to start writing.

Every story starts with an idea.

You may already know exactly what you want to write about. Maybe you have too many ideas and can't choose or maybe you have no idea at all. It doesn't matter because we're starting from scratch. And I'll tell you this upfront: your story WILL change, many times, throughout the process.

I don't tell you this to discourage you. Contrary, I see it as a beautiful path of an unfolding discovery that can only be found through the writing process. So don't feel overwhelmed or frustrated by this. Instead, see it as necessary for the story to shape itself into what it's meant to be. The story idea you come up with now is allowed to change, and often is required to, before you reach the end. It's just part of the process.

One more thing before you get into discovering your story: you are not writing this story alone, nor should you ever believe that you are.

When you write from the idea that you have to come up with all of it yourself, you write from a place of ego which we've learned is the place in the head where only limited and negative thinking exist. It's much more magnificent than you can imagine. All you have to do is open yourself to guidance from your Highest Self, from the Divine, from the Universe—whatever you'd like to call it—and allow the words to flow through you.

Take no credit for what you write because you are only the vessel for the message to be delivered to our physical world, and YOU, with your personal experiences, are the only one who can convert the message, or story, as it's meant to be told. But you are not the only one writing it. Something bigger than you is at work here. Work with it, rather than against it, and you'll find nothing but ease and joy in the writing process. That's exactly how I'm writing this book, and how I wrote my last novel, *The Raven Wars*. It's no wonder I've written both so quickly when you understand that I'm not doing this alone. I have guidance. I'm in awe through most of it because of the imagination that pours through me to bring a string of words together to create something magical. It feels so personal, yet so universal.

This is the place you want to be in when you write. Start each writing session with a short intention. Get quiet, connect within and ask for guidance in your writing session. You'll be amazed at what, or who, comes to your aid.

DISCOVERING YOUR STORY

Theme: It's pretty well-known that all great stories have a theme. In _The Lord of the Rings_ the theme is something like naiveté to worldliness. Frodo Baggins is forced to leave the Shire when he's given a ring that threatens all of Middle Earth. He starts out happy and innocent in this journey, not really aware of what's against him because he's been sheltered in the Shire his entire life. But by the end of the story, he's survived so much that he now sees that world for what it is, both beauty and terror, and he understands much more about the purpose of his journey.

A theme sets the tone for the story. It gives the bare bones of a structure for you to work with. You will know where the story will start and where it will end, based on the protagonist's (main character's) internal journey.

Pivotal Moment: These are moments in a story, or moments in our lives that create big change, either within or without, and usually create a negative experience or feeling.

This is where the foundations we set in the first half of this book will prove invaluable. You will create the _Theme_ for your story right now by discovering _Pivotal Moments_ from your own life that you want to use as possible story ideas. So you see, it's essential that you're living from the _internal writer's journey_ as you go through this process, otherwise it can feel quite impossible or intimidating. Return to the _Moving From Your Head Into Your Mind_ section for a refresh if you need to before you move on. Approach these next steps with a quiet mind and faith that you can do this.

So let's start now.

I suggest you use a journal or Word Document that you will return to throughout this process. Get quiet, intend to be at peace as you go through this. Close your eyes if you need to. Just sit quietly for a few minutes, breathing deeply.

Find three moments in your life that left you or your life changed, preferably a difficult time as this is where a good story begins—with a struggle or challenge that must be overcome. Don't overthink this. There will be far more than three moments that come to mind, but trust your intuition to guide you to the three that you're meant to address right now, to turn into a story that will change you and those who read it. What stories came to you during the quiet? Take some time now, before moving on, to write them down so you don't forget. Keep them safe because you will use them throughout this journey. You can type them up in a separate word document or write them in your journal.

Once you've written all three moments down, follow the steps here:

1. Of the pivotal moments you uncovered, which ONE is the most impactful for you? This will be the focus of your story idea as you move forward. The other pivotal moments will be used along the journey too, but you want ONE to focus on.

2. What emotions come up for you when you think back to this moment in time? (anger, guilt, shame, sadness, unworthiness, frustration, disappointment, etc.) First list them all out. Then, circle the ONE emotion that feels the most powerful to you. Finally, think of the ONE emotion that is the opposite of this negative emotion (lightness, self-love, acceptance, freedom, etc). These two emotions will be the overall THEME of your story. (Example: Shame to Self-Love)

3. What are some ideas for a story that surround the emotions and experiences that you went through

during this time in your life? What's important here is to separate the story from yourself so you can let go of any judgements you're holding on to around this moment.

The two emotions you wrote down at the end, one negative and one positive, are the *Theme* of your story! This *Theme* is also the fuel for your story idea. All you need to do is use your imagination. Let it flow freely here and see what ideas come. Write any story ideas that come to you now, keep them brief, and follow your instinct on the one that feels most right to you. This *Theme* and story idea will be what your novel will be about.

With your Theme and story idea in place, it's time to move forward to create some characters and the setting for your story.

Genre, Setting, Characters, And You

As we already discussed, it's entirely up to you whether you plan or outline your book ahead of time, or jump right into writing it. If you're ready to start writing with the story idea you've come up with, then go for it! The characters and story will unfold as you go if you keep faith that they will.

If you want some planning, then you can use the following as a general guide to decide on what genre and setting your book will have, and who the characters will be. I personally plan a bit before I write. Once I have a clear story idea, I jump right into planning a few of the characters—mainly the protagonist, antagonist, and supporting characters to the protagonist. That's it. The other characters come to me as I write and the story unfolds.

But, you can do this in any way you'd like! That's the beauty of the *internal writer's journey*. You trust your intuition and do what feels right to you. If you feel better understanding all the characters in your story before you write a word, then begin visualizing them. I have some tips you can use as guidance on creating your characters below.

Again, the choice is yours! Go within and listen to your intuition.

To be clear, you're using pivotal moments from your own life, therefore the story you're about to write is your journey rewritten through a fictional lens and focused on the emotional journey you went through during that time of your life. This means that as you create characters and setting, they will also come from your actual life (write what you know and tell the truth, as Stephen King said)—only, you will want to shift them around so that you're not giving a literal retelling of your life.

Let's take a look at how you can explore the genre, setting, and characters for your novel by using your own experiences in time and space, the people who were part of your pivotal moments, but also using your imagination to make it creative for your story.

Genre

Genre is important because it tells the readers what to expect if they decide to pick up your book. It will determine what type of cover you have, and who you will promote it to. Knowing your genre before you begin writing will save you a lot of unnecessary effort because you will already know what's expected of your story. I suggest that you choose a genre you're already familiar with and one that you greatly enjoy.

For example, I've loved fantasy stories my entire life. I consume them in all mediums, even as an adult. So what genre do I write in? Fantasy!

As I started creating my stories, I found that I already intuitively knew the flow the story should take and expectations readers would have because I was a reader of these types of stories, and I knew what my expectations were of other fantasy stories. I did little research on how to write Fantasy, but instead practiced the *internal writer's journey*—I got quiet, meditated on the story I was meant to tell, and intended that it would be so—and as soon as I committed to sitting down to write, the story just came to me in floods.

The same can be for you if you stick to what you already know and love and then practice the *internal writer's journey* with confidence and faith. Decide on your genre now and write it down where you wrote out your pivotal moments.

Some common genres are: Sci-Fi, Fantasy, Magical Realism, Romance, Literary Fiction, Horror, Thriller, Mystery. There are more, but these are just a few. Please get clear on what the genre of your favorite stories are to help you decide which one you will choose.

Setting

Think back to your pivotal moments. Where did they take place? Where were you at emotionally while they were happening? Specifically the pivotal moment that you chose as your story idea—the one you created your Theme with. Write out the scene or scenes of what it looked like and felt like in those moments, whether it was one quick moment or several long drawn out moments. Writing them out will allow you to see them from a different point of view—one where you're no longer the victim but an observer.

Once you have those scenes written in your own word, whether a few sentences, several paragraphs, or many pages doesn't matter, let your imagination take over. How can you shift these places from your own life experiences into places that belong in the genre you chose?

For example, in my novel, *The Wonder Soul*, I placed my

protagonist in San Diego at the beginning of the book—which is where I live and where all of my pivotal moments took place. However, I moved the location to a different place in San Diego from where each moment really happened. And shortly after the beginning of the book, the setting moves to San Francisco, then Ireland, and Greece. I've not been to any of these places! But for the story I wanted to tell—magical realism focused on reconnecting with the child-like wonder within—I knew that having the main character travel to some magical places would be fitting.

Answering these questions may help you get more clarity around your setting:

- What type of story are you writing? What Genre are you writing in? For example, if you're writing Sci-Fi or Fantasy type of story, you can really explore the setting with an entirely new world or race of beings that make it a lot of fun to explore your pivotal moments, emotional journey, and Theme within them. (This is what I did in The Raven Dreams Series). If your story is more grounded in reality as we know it, such as Romance or Mystery, then it will take place in the real world, but it may—for example—take place across the world from where you were at. Get creative.
- Now, reflect on the emotional journey of your protagonist (YOU). Think about the Theme of your story. What type of setting would best suit this journey in your mind?

Take your time with this. There's no rush! Take hours or day, but don't put it off too long so that it never gets done. All you need is a few lines stating what you would like your setting to be, or where you would like your story to take place.

Characters

As you rewrite moments from your own life into the fictional story that will be your novel, you might think of people who were in your life during those times, and how you can include them without hurting anyone's feelings or without them finding out you wrote a story about them. **First, let me say that this is YOUR story and no one else's opinion should matter, nor does anyone ever has to see it if you don't want them to.** But if you do plan to share or publish this story at some point, it's important to be respectful while still being truthful. This section is designed to help you come up with characters without "calling people out" from your pivotal moments.

It's common to believe that to create a character, you simply need to decide on what kind of personality they will have, and you're all set. But, your characters need much more than a personality. You want them to be four-dimensional, like they come alive on the page, and if you only give them a personality, they will fall flat. The readers will not resonate with them. So how do you make them four-dimensional?

Characters need a distinct *attitude* and *worldview* that is unique to them. You can define a character's attitude clearly by <u>understanding who they are</u> and <u>what they've done</u>, which shapes their self-perception (how they see themselves and what they think of themselves), and their perception of the world— or their worldview. So, to understand a character's worldview, you must first get clear on their attitude. Personality will also fall into place as you get clear on the individual attitude.

And keep in mind, that the protagonist, or hero, of your story is YOU because you're using moments from your own life to write this story. It only makes sense that you place yourself at the center of the story. You want your protagonist to embody you without being a literal reincarnation of you.

Protagonist/Hero

Recall the Theme you uncovered based on the emotions of your main pivotal moment. How can you shape your protagonist's (YOUR) inner world at the start of the story based on this knowledge?

What will be the protagonist's (YOUR) perception of their outer world be based on this inner state of being? Think back to yourself at this time and how you perceived your outer world.

Get deep. You'll want to tap into parts of yourself during these pivotal moments that weren't so pleasant, so that you can both create a powerful emotional journey for the story, AND you will find healing through this process too. Be creative on ways you can show the same emotions through different internal and external lenses of your protagonist.

If they were stranded on a desert island, what 3 things would they want to have?

If they heard a noise in the dead of the night, how would they react? What happened at a young age to create this fear?

Create a name and physical traits for your hero that resonate with you.

Antagonist/Villain:

First decide, will your antagonist be a person, place, thing, emotion, concept, societal norm, etc. Write down what form your antagonist will take.

Now, how will the antagonist challenge your hero (YOU) throughout the story? Will it be direct or indirect? Will it be an extreme violation of the hero's being, or more subtle and slow? How will the antagonist create mayhem for your hero?

Create a name (and physical traits, if applicable) for the antagonist that will be easy to reference from the start of the story.

Additional Characters:

List out all the people who were in your life during your pivotal moments.

Next, choose at least three of these people to include in your story. The ones that will evoke the most emotion and directly played a part in the story. There's no right amount but going through at least three people with this exercise will benefit you and your story whether or not you decide to include them. If you have more, great!

Answer the following about them:

- Physical Traits
- Personality Traits

- **Attitude** and **Worldview**
- Emotions you feel when you think about them
- Were they positive or negative during the pivotal moments of your life?
- Create a name for each one

I know this seems like a lot right now. Take it one step at a time, one day at a time. The process cannot, and will not be rushed. If you like to set goals, set one that feels good to you to complete this. Otherwise, just go through it bits at a time, or complete it all in one sitting!

You may have chosen not to use any of this and instead use your intuition entirely as you sit down and write your story purely from the story idea you created. That's perfect too, as long as it *feels* good to you!

I want to take a moment here to return to the foundations we built in the first half of this book. I know from experience in my own writing journey that this is the moment your faith is tested and your dream to write a novel is threatened. The entire first half of this book, I encouraged the idea that you must live the *internal writer's journey* if you want to write the book that only you can write, the one that will inspire and impact both your readers and yourself. That looks like getting quiet, meditating, holding an intention, and sitting down to write. Right now, you're at the sitting down to write part of the process, and I've just shared a good amount of guidance for you to follow should you choose to.

But I want you to always return to getting quiet, meditating, and holding *your* intentions for *your* novel. It's from that place that you will stay centered on what feels good to you. Some steps above may not feel good for you and that's okay! Skip them. Take what works for you and leave the rest.

I only hope to give you another way to write your book—one that is focused within rather than without. How you choose to use it is your decision and never forget that. Once you feel ready to move on, turn the page to continue on where we will take a deeper look at how your story will unfold.

The Two
Hero's Journeys

You may have heard of Joseph Campbell. He created the Hero's Journey which is twelve stages of a journey that stories take, whether in fictional storytelling or in our own lives. In his book, *The Hero With A Thousand Faces*, Campbell outlines a universal motif of adventure and transformation that runs through virtually all the world's mythic traditions. This is the Hero's Journey. And we'll go over it in detail below. But first, I want to talk about the two hero's journeys. This statement is twofold.

There are two hero's journeys: internal and external. And there are two hero's journeys: yours and your protagonist's.

Let's take a look at the *internal journey* and *external journey* of the two hero's journeys first. You are already well acquainted with the concept of internal and external journeys since we talked about them in depth in Part 2 of this book. This idea mirrors your story because your main character, or protagonist, will have to embark on a journey for there to be a compelling story, and this journey will be both internal and external. Your character will both have to face and overcome things in their external world, while digesting and reacting internally to everything that happens. This second part is very emotional.

The good new is, you already know what the *internal journey* of your protagonist will be. It's the Theme you discovered a short while ago. Like in the example I gave of Frodo Baggins, his internal journey is one from Naiveté to Worldliness. The two emotions you decided on will be the internal journey your character will experience in your story. You may be beginning to see now how creating your story idea from your own life experiences and creating everything that follows based on these moments allows you to write your story purely from within. And it's all connected—your life to the story, internal to external, you to the character.

That's the beauty of the internal writer's journey!

You can write down the *internal journey* your character will go on in the story, and you may already have some ideas of how she will get from Point A (or naiveté) to Point B (or worldliness). Your Point A and Point B will be unique to your own Theme and internal journey. Take some time to write down a couple of different paths your protagonist (you) can take to get from Point A to Point B.

Next, you want to spend a few minutes deciding on the external journey of your character. What will they have to face in their physical world? Bu we'll return to this in a moment. First, I want to explain the other hero's journeys.

The other two hero's journeys are yours and your protagonist's. Your protagonist's hero's journey will be the same as the *external journey* which we will talk about in a moment. Your hero's journey, I'm sure you've guessed, is that pivotal moment you wrote down that became your story idea. But more than that, it's everything in between all the pivotal moments you wrote. You can pull from those other moments to help you build the journey for your character, which is the same as building the story.

So really, the only thing you have to create here is the *external journey*, also known as your protagonist's hero's journey! Because you already have a good idea of what the *internal (emotional) journey* will look like, and you already know your own journey very well. That being said, let's take a look at the Hero's Journey as outlined by Joseph Campbell. I've broken them into the twelve stages and summarized each on in my own words:

1. *Ordinary World*
   This is where the hero exists before the story begins. It's his safe place. This is his/her everyday life where we learn about his/her true nature and capabilities.

2. *Call to Adventure*
   This can be a direct threat to him/her or the family, or community. It will disrupt the comfort of the hero's Ordinary World and present a challenge that must be undertaken.

3. *Refusal of the Call*
   The hero has fears he needs to overcome before he/she can accept the Call to Adventure. Until that moment, he/she will refuse the call. As a result of the refusal, he/she may suffer somehow.

4. *Meeting with the Mentor*
   The hero meets a mentor who gives him/her something he/she needs, whether physical,

spiritual or emotional. This will dispel his/her fears and doubts and give him/her the courage to begin the adventure.

5. *Crossing the Threshold*
   The hero may go willingly or may be pushed over the threshold between his Ordinary World and the Magical World. This can mean leaving home for the first time or doing something he's/she's always been afraid to do.

6. *Tests, Allies, Enemies*
   Now the hero is out of his/her comfort zone and he will need to find out who can be trusted and who can't. Each person/event (good or bad), in their own way, will prepare him/her for what's to come.

7. *Approach to the Inmost Cave*
   This may be an actual location in which lies a terrible danger, or it may be an inner conflict which up until now the hero has avoided facing.

8. *Ordeal, death, rebirth*
   The ordeal is a dangerous test or a deep inner battle the hero must face in order to survive. Only through some form of "death" can the hero be reborn in a metaphorical resurrection that somehow grants him/her greater power to do what he needs to do.

9. *Reward/Seizing the Sword*

   After defeating the enemy, surviving death and finally overcoming his/her greatest personal challenge, the hero is rewarded: an object of great importance or power, a secret, greater knowledge or insight, or even reconciliation with a loved one or ally.

10. *The Road Back*

    Now he/she must return home with his/her reward. The moment before the hero finally commits to the last stage of his/her journey may be a moment in which he/she must choose between his/her own personal objective and that of a Higher Cause.

11. *Resurrection/Final Battle*

    This is the climax in which the hero must have his/her final and most dangerous encounter with death. The final battle also represents something far greater than the hero's own existence with its outcome having far-reaching consequences to his Ordinary World and the lives of those he/she left behind.

12. *Return with the Elixir*

    This is the final stage of the Hero's journey in which he/she returns home to his/her Ordinary World a changed person. He/She will have grown as a person, learned many things, faced many terrible dangers

and even death but now looks forward to
the start of a new life.

At this moment, I want you to pause, take a deep breath, and go within. Set the book down, get quiet, and ask yourself . . . *Do I want to use this as an outline for my book before I start writing?*

Did you do it? Good. Because only you can decide how to use the Hero's Journey to aid you in your writing process. What's important is that you now have it, should you decide to use it. I would recommend that you at lease visit it before you write, or as you write, because it will help you build a compelling story. It will save you so much guess work because Campbell already did the work for you. All you have to do is fill in the blanks to make them right for your story!

Each of the twelve stages is broken down into The Beginning, The Middle, or The End of your story. I gauge it as follows: Stages 1-4 take place in The Beginning, Stages 5-9 take place in The Middle, and Stages 10-12 are The End. Keep in mind that each stage will be one scene or a few scenes of your novel, not your entire novel. There will be many scenes to write in between these twelve stages.

This is how I use the Hero's Journey to outline my story. I write one or two sentences for each stage based on what I already know of my pivotal moments, theme, and internal journey of my character. Also based on what type of characters I created. That's it! I simply write a couple of sentences for each stage so I can see the flow of my story on one page.

Take some time now to figure out what these twelves stage look like for your story. Remember to stay centered within, listening to that quiet voice that's guiding you. You aren't writing this book alone, but you're simply the vessel being guided to put the words to paper. Trust in the process and in your higher power.

Before we move on, here are the aspects of your story you want to get really clear on based on what we've talked about here: the internal journey of your character, which is also the Theme of your story; the external journey of your character, which is also the Hero's Journey outlined above. Your pivotal moments will highly influence the internal journey and external journey your main character takes (this is combining your journey with your own journey).

In Part 4 of this book, we will go through bringing all of this together, so for now, just take notes in a way that are easy for you to make sense of and keep track of. Outline if you would like, using the twelve stages of the Hero's Journey, or use whatever method feels good to you. We have one more idea to discuss before getting into the hardcore writing of your novel.

The Parts Of Story

Now you're starting to see your story unfold into a book. You've created the story idea based around a pivotal moment of your own life, which also gave you the Theme, or *internal (emotional) journey* of your character and story. You have a vision for the genre and setting, and you've created characters that will come to life on the page. The Hero's Journey gave you an external picture of the *external journey* your protagonist will take based on both the twelve stages and your own personal journey.

Now, it's time to look at the five parts of a story that bring it all together and give it that extra magic!

Inciting Incident
Progressive Complications
Crisis
Climax
Resolution

You may have heard of these before. They are quite well known in the writing world and talked about often. I personally like to use Sean Coyne's take on these five parts of story, or as he calls them the <u>5 Commandments of Story</u>.

Sean Coyne is the creator of the Story Grid Method, as well as an editor of over twenty-five years. The reason I like to use his method is that he gets this *internal writer's journey*, which we've spent a lot of time talking about in this book. He understands everyone has to find what works for them, and that's how he teaches. Much of my confidence as a writer has come from using his method in my own work, but keeping it true to how I want to write.

So, the 5 Commandments of Story. This is the last step for our purposes of finding the story you're meant to write. Let's look at them each individually.

Inciting Incident

This kicks the story off with some excitement. Most of the time, this will be the moment that kick-started your pivotal moment. You want to use your imagination to create a fictional story with a protagonist (main character) that represents you, but is not you. The same goes for the events. Have fun with them and get creative on ways you can show the inciting incident (your pivotal moment) through a fictional lens.

Progressive Complications

The protagonist encounters these throughout the story and they will try to throw her off her original journey. They are a series of roadblocks and lead to the Crisis. This can be anything that presented you with a challenge after your pivotal moment (inciting incident) took place. What was the snowball effect? Limiting beliefs that created complications? External factors that created complications?

Crisis

This is the do-or-die moment where the protagonist has to gather all their strength in one final effort to defeat the antagonist. This is the moment you felt all was lost. Here, your character will have to choose a "best bad decision". The pivotal moment in your life has taken control and you have to find a way to continue on even though it seems impossible.

Climax

This is the beginning of your (your character's) breakthrough when you realize even in the face of certain death, you can rise above—the peak of the story towards the end; a big action scene or revelation.

Resolution

You've made it through the eye of the storm. This moment of your life is behind you and you can now look back on it as a new, stronger person. Tie up loose ends; resolve character's initial problem.

Just like the Hero's Journey in the previous section, you will use all you've built around your pivotal moment so far to fill in what each of these 5 Commandments will be for your story. Don't overthink it. Just go with what feels right to you now. It may change later, and that's okay. It doesn't matter if they change from what you write today. It only matters that each of these are in your story and well thought out. Remember not to rush, or pressure yourself to be perfect.

Write a few sentences for each one, or notes around ideas that come to you for each of these commandments. In the next part of this book, we will bring it all together so you will see how each piece of story we've talked about fits together and you can begin writing your draft. So don't worry if you feel confused or overwhelmed. Remember, this is exactly where we don't want to be. If you're feeling that now, step away, go meditate or take a walk and clear your head. Come back when you're ready to move forward.

If you stay on the path of the *internal writer's journey* it will all come to you if you just allow it to.

Part 4

Bringing It All Together to Write Your Novel

The Beginning

In the previous part of this book, you spent time cultivating the story for your book. And most importantly, you did it from the inside-out, following the *internal writer's journey*. If you also implemented the foundations we talked about at the beginning of this book, you've found that your intuition is really all you need to write your book. If you only allow it too, your intuition will step in and let you know what feels right and what doesn't for your story. There's no need to search "how-to" information online, join a writing group to get opinions, or look anywhere outside of yourself for the answers of how to write your book.

You have all you need.

All I've done in the previous pages was to share with you how I shifted from the external to the internal and what that looks like for me when I write my books. You are not obligated to follow every step I've shared here. If you know of another way, or if another way comes to you in the process, trust it. I'm only sharing what I know with you to give you guidance should you need it, and you won't hurt my feelings if you choose not to use some, or any, of what I've shared here. I trust that if you're in alignment with your

Highest Self and you're allowing the story to flow through you, that you have all you need.

That being said, it's time to get in even deeper into writing your novel if you haven't already begun. And we're going to start at the beginning! If there's one thing all human beings can agree on, it's that every good story has a beginning, middle, and end. If it were missing any one of these, it wouldn't be a story but a fragment of one. While you can choose to start anywhere you'd like in your story— as long as you complete all of it in the end—I like to start at the beginning. It's just the natural flow for me to write the story from start to finish, though some writers do enjoy writing the ending, or even the scenes they're most excited about writing, first.

You can do it however you like!

I suggest you recenter before you go any further. Return to that inner space, to your Highest Self. Get quiet, meditate, hold an intention for what you want your book to be. And when you're ready, come back here to see how to bring everything you've already created together and make it into one magical story.

The way I've broken this down is by using the stages of the Hero's Journey (*external journey*), as well as the stages of the character's *internal journey* as I have interpreted them through my own writing. If you've already written some sentences for each of the twelve stages of the Hero's Journey, then you're ahead of the game because you already know where your story is going.

They key in writing the story is to bring the *internal and external journeys* of your character together and create them into scenes that then come together to create chapters.

But right now, we're only looking at the beginning of

your story. The first four stages of the Hero's Journey will be used here. Here they are again:

- (1) Ordinary World
- (2) Call to Adventure
- (3) Refusal of the Call
- (4) Meeting the Mentor

So these are the first stages what you really want to flesh out. Go back to those sentences you wrote for each one and write as much as you can for each until there's nothing more. You will come back to add more later, so don't worry if you think it's too short. Your focus now is to get a first draft written. It's in the second or third draft that you expand and refine. Right now, just let it be what it is, and let it be messy.

So go ahead and flesh out each of these stages as much as you can. Turn the sentences into scenes, add more scenes and ideas, build the characters, create interactions and dialogue. Take your time and come back when you're ready to move forward.

[Note: A scene is simply a piece of a story. It can vary in length. Some scenes are 500 words, others are 2500 words. Don't worry about how long they are, just let them be as they are and trust that it's good for now. Scene length can also vary depending on how long your entire novel is. All you need to know is a scene is a piece of the story. Alone, they are only a fragment, but once you've written all the scenes and put them together, they create an entire novel. In *Lord of the Rings*, a scene example is the moment at the end of the story when Frodo and Sam are in Mount Doom, Frodo suddenly doesn't want to destroy the ring, they get ambushed by Gollum, and then Gollum is thrown over the edge along with the ring. That's one piece of the entire story, or one scene.]

The other key element you want to include in the beginning of your story is the *inciting incident*. If you remember, this is the first of the 5 Commandments of Story. It's the event or moment that kicks off the story—it's also the pivotal moment you chose to work with. This usually happens fairly quickly in stories because this is the moment that will catch the reader's attention and make them want to keep reading to see what happens. The other four commandments will come later. Right now, we only need to flesh out the inciting incident.

For me, the inciting incident in *Lord of the Rings* (Fellowship) is the moment when Frodo learns of the one ring and Gandalf tells him that he must be the one to destroy it. It's possible the J. R. R. Tolkien had another moment in mind as the inciting incident when he wrote the book, but we'll never know. It can vary for each person as a reader because we all come from different walks of life and experiences so what may feel like an inciting incident to one person may be different from the actual inciting incident as intended by the author.

And that's okay!

That's the beauty of story. It's open for interpretation for each individual to enjoy however they will. Your only job is to make sure you write the best inciting incident you can and then leave it be. I often find that the inciting incident falls in nicely with the Call to Adventure (Stage 2 of The Hero's Journey). It allows some time to introduce your world and your characters, to show what your protagonist's life is like through an ordinary lens. And then things are shaken up with the call to adventure!

Go back to your Call to Adventure and check if you already wrote the inciting incident intuitively. If not, take some time now and add it into this part of your story.

The next thing to keep in mind is the *internal (emotional) journey* your character is going through while embarking on their *external journey*. If you need some guidance with this, here are some prompts and questions to help you, mixed in with the stages of the Hero's Journey and 5 Commandments of Story:

> Where is your protagonist at emotionally when the story begins? Think back to how you felt in your own world right before your pivotal moment took place. Show what they think and feel, interact with the people and environment around them. (Ordinary World)

> How will your protagonist react to the inciting incident which will tempt them to leave their world behind, or be led away by a calling—person, place or thing that calls to them? (Call to Adventure)

> How will the protagonist's reaction affect the other characters in the story, directly or indirectly)?

> What internal struggles is the protagonist dealing with after the Inciting Incident? What prompts them to reject the challenge? (Refuses the Call)

> What do they hope to accomplish by rejecting the challenge? What is their desired outcome by rejecting the challenge?

> Who or what will come into their life to
> change their mind and accept the challenge
> presented? (Meeting the Mentor)

There's a lot to write and explore here, so don't rush it. Trust in yourself and the process. Believe that you are not alone writing this story, but that you are simply the vessel through which the story is to be told, but there are higher forces at work with you, guiding you along every step of the way. Always return to your notes about character and setting, Theme and Hero's Journey, and the 5 Commandments. They work together to build your entire story. Continue to The Middle once you feel you've written as much of The Beginning of your story as possible.

The Middle

Before we move onto the middle of your story, I must warn you . . . this is the place where most people give up. The excitement they had at The Beginning of the story is gone and the work has set in. The Middle of the story is the longest. It's the easiest place to lose momentum because you can't see the end in sight. This is the time where you have to break through the resistance that will inevitably come to stop you from sitting down to write.

I face this challenge every single time.

The difference is, that I now know how to work through it, even embrace it, so that I can let go and keep going. The *internal writer's journey* once again is key here. If you're connected to the story at a spiritual and emotional level (now you see why we used your own life to inspire the storyline of your novel), then it gives you the inspiration you need to keep going—even if you take a day off, or a couple of days— it's what will bring you back to your chair to keep writing.

Steven Pressfield is masterful at describing resistance. He wrote an entire book on it—*The War of Art*. If you don't have a copy, I highly recommend you get one. It's an easy read, and it really works to flip to any page on any day and use that as your guidance to keep going when you want to give up. It's not a book you have to read from start to finish, though I have, and now I revisit whatever page comes up for me in the moment as inspiration for my creative journey.

"Rule of thumb: The more important a call or action is to our soul's evolution, the more Resistance we will feel toward pursuing it."— Steven Pressfield

So now you've been warned. You're aware of the inevitable resistance that's on its way to you, if it hasn't already knocked on your door. Just know, that it happens to everyone. As Steven Pressfield says, the more important the calling, the higher the resistance. Shift your perspective on the resistance, and it will melt away. See it as a blessing, rather than a curse, that you're on the right track purely from the fact that resistance has shown up.

Staying on your path of the *internal writer's journey* will also help lessen the resistance. Stay true to you. Don't stray or be tempted by the opinions of the outside world in these moments you want to quit. Instead, get quiet and go within to ask for guidance out of the resistance.

Okay, on to the middle of your story!

We're moving onto stages 5 through 9 of the Hero's Journey. Here they are:

- (5) Crossing the Threshold
- (6) Tests, Allies, Enemies
- (7) Approach/Preparation
- (8) Ordeal, Death (Metaphorical), Rebirth
- (9) Reward/Seizing the Sword

In the middle of the story is a good place to add some *progressive complications* (Commandment 2). These are the roadblocks and challenges your protagonist will have to overcome to grow into that end goal you set in place with the Theme (i.e. Naiveté to Worldliness). You want the story to end with him/her achieving that worldliness, but he/she can't unless he/she grows through the story. That's what the progressive complications provide. Notice the word "progressive" implies that they will progress in difficulty as the story progresses.

There is no right or wrong place to add these into your story. No right or wrong to how many progressive complications you create. It's unique to you and your story. Go within to find the answer for you. I don't worry about it in anymore, but just write and I find they come as needed.

Again, you'll return to the sentences you wrote for each stage of the Hero's Journey (5-9) and flesh them out. Stop here to do that now, even if it's days or weeks until you're ready to pick up the book again. Keep faith and keep going. You know what you need to do. The story is unfolding just as it wants to.

Here are some prompts and questions to guide you if needed:

> What does your protagonist hope to accomplish now that they've accepted the challenge and entered the special world? What problems will they face along the journey of taking action? Trials can be a person, situation, worldview or concept. Ex. Hero is physically attacked by another, hero falls into a cavernous cave, hero is confronted with a dark memory from their past, etc. (Crossing the Threshold)

> This would be a good spot to intertwine your second pivotal moment. It can be

a sentence or two. It doesn't have to be lengthy. Just powerful.

What tests, allies or enemies does your hero encounter? As with trials, tests, allies, and enemies can by physical people, a situation, or a concept/worldview. (Tests, Allies, Enemies)

How do they help her/him grow in a positive way, or generate more self-doubt within her/him? (Approach-Preparation)

What will be the ultimate evil that knocks your hero off their game? Again, a physical evil enemy, a dark situation in her/his life that comes up, or something that turns her/him against herself can all be types of evil. (Ordeal)

This would be a good time to tie in the third pivotal moment you wrote down to the rest of the story. It can be a sentence or two. It doesn't have to be lengthy. Just powerful.

How will her/his defeat make her feel? How will her/his reaction affect the allies that have come into her life? Really *feel* your protagonist's emotion here and show it on the page. (Death)

What consequences come from the choices made, and the actions taken, and how do these help your hero see themselves in a new light? How will these consequences affect the world your hero lives in? (Rebirth)

What leap of faith does your hero take that will ultimately lead to defeating the evil? (Seizing the Sword)

Return to the foundations at the beginning of this book. Stay centered on your *internal writer's journey* and keep faith. Take as much time as you need to write the middle of your book, knowing that when you're ready, you can return and the end will be waiting for you. It's not going anywhere.

The End

Congratulations! You've made it through the longest part of your story. I hope you're beginning to see the light at the end of the tunnel. You still have a big task ahead of you, because the ending is the most important part of the story. It's the payoff, the transformation. Your character has been through so much already but there's still a lot to overcome before the end.

The same goes for you as the writer.

The truth is, when working from the *internal writer's journey*, none of this should seem hard. There will be setbacks, struggles even, but the entire process will feel joyful and exciting if you're operating from within, rather than without. You'll be able to see all of it as perfect and beautiful for your end goal, even if it doesn't turn out how you envisioned it would.

Resistance will have reared its head at you so many times now, you've mastered the art of taming it and taking back control of your creative process. This gives you a new confidence in your writing. Rest assured, the resistance will never stop, but your faith in your ability to keep it at bay will grow stronger each time you continue despite the resistance.

It's now time to write the end of your story.

Here you will write the last three stages of the Hero's Journey, as well as the last three commandments. Let's start with the Hero's Journey stages:

- (10) The Road Back
- (11) Resurrection/Final Battle
- (12) Return with the Elixir

Here are the remaining three Commandments of Story *(Note: You will also still have Progressive Complications throughout the story until you reach the resolution)*:

- Crisis
- Climax
- Resolution

There is no right or wrong as to how you intermix these. The only structure to follow here is the sequential order of each group. For instance, you don't want to put the climax before the crisis, or Stage 12 of the Hero's Journey before Stage 10. If you find that your crisis is occurring between The Road Back and Resurrection, then let it be there. If your climax and resolution fall within the Return with the Elixir, that's right for you.

Don't overthink. Let your intuition and higher power guide you.

Pause here, revisit the sentences your wrote, and write out the scenes for each of these stages until you're satisfied.

Here are the prompts and questions to further help you:

> After taking the leap of faith or facing the
> consequences now apparent in their world,

what complications will your hero have to overcome? (The Road Back)

What will your protagonist and those in their life have to choose between because of these complications? Feeling torn between the two choices is the crisis. The choice your hero makes here determines their fate. (The Road Back)

What does the choice your protagonist made say about who they really are? This reveal is the climax. After the battle (literal or metaphorical), how does the student (your hero) become the teacher?—Resolution. (Resurrection/Final Battle)

What is she feeling emotionally after conquering the evil? Often a bittersweet experience.

Show the transformation and how they've changed since the story started. (Return with the Elixir)

Wrap up the story either by tying up the loose ends or leaving it open ended.

Take a deep breath in . . . and exhale. You've got this. If you've been doing the work as we've been going, then know that you're so close. Don't give up now. Don't even think about it. As soon as your draft is done, you can celebrate!

If you've chosen to read the entire book before starting

(I get it, I do the same thing!), then I hope you can see the whole picture now of what lies ahead of you. It's a lot of work, no doubt, but it's well worth it and both you and those who will read your book—should you publish it—will be changed for the better because of it.

Yes, there's still work ahead of you. The first draft is done and now is time for rest. Walk away from your book for a while—at least a week—and come back with fresh eyes. In the following section, I will offer guidance on your next steps.

What Next?

Whether you've written as you've read this book, or you're reading it all the way through before you begin, you will have some questions at this point. I've guided you through my entire process of writing my first draft using the internal writer's journey. This is how I do it, and all I do.

You might be wondering if I've left some things out, or noticed I have left some things out that you've heard others say are necessary for writing a first draft. The truth is, that's their opinion—and we've already talked about what living by the opinions of others will do, not just to your writing, but your life. What I've given you here are the bare essentials for you to write your first draft. It is up to you to fill in the blanks using anything that feels good to you.

You may be worrying about things such as: *What is a scene exactly, and how do I write one? Am I understanding the 5 Commandments of Story correctly and writing them as I should be? How can I possibly fill in the blanks between the stages that were given to me and write an entire novel, start to finish? Am I writing enough words; is my book the "right" length?*

If you're in this place right now, calmly remind yourself you're operating from the *external writer's journey* where fear, doubt, and overwhelm have control over you. Return to the foundations of this book. Read them over as many times as you need to, and most importantly, practice them as often as possible until you become the writer who trusts only your intuition, who has faith and confidence to know you have all the answers within you to write your book.

As soon as you question whether you're doing it "right", you've stepped back into the external path and you're focused on the people, opinions, and experiences of things outside of yourself. There is nothing to question except your inner guide—your Highest Self, that Divine Source within you which is also part of you—when you feel you've lost momentum, or you're experiencing writer's block, or fear creeps into your mind.

This is the time to get quiet and return to your meditation, holding the intentions for what you want this book to be. See it as if it's already written and feel what that feels like to you. Then have complete faith that it is so, and you are being guided to complete your book in just that way.

The *internal writer's journey* is very freeing as soon as you're willing to step into it completely. It's a path where you no longer have to doubt yourself or your process. The opinion's of others can be valuable at times, but they aren't necessary for you to sit down and do the work. Resistance falls into the shadows as your light begins to shine so brightly there's room for nothing other than your Divine Self who is in control, yet also guided by that higher Universal force that works through everyone.

The biggest challenge is getting to that place.

But if you're persistent, and you keep faith that you are that author, you are on the *internal writer's journey*, there will come a day when you're writing and it hits you with a wave of inspiration and goosebumps—you ARE that author.

What's next on this journey once you've written a first draft?

Writing a complete draft is a HUGE accomplishment that most who set out to write a novel never reach. Now is a time to celebrate and feel the gratitude for what you've done. But the book is not done. There is more writing to do, revisions, and edits. The focus of this book is to get yourself out of your own way to write the book. So I won't get too deep into the rest of the stages, but I will offer you guidance based on what I do.

First, when you feel you've written all you can toward your draft, it's time to look at the story itself and see if it works based on the genre you chose. When I say "see if it works", I mean it's written to inspire and impact readers who are lovers of that genre. Thankfully, there is a method available to you to uncover this for your own story, and it's called the *Story Grid*, by Sean Coyne.

I have to be upfront in saying the Story Grid will not be for everyone. It can get analytical, but there are so many free resources available to you to help you take your own book through the Story Grid, so it's worth at least trying it. I personally love switching from the creative and imaginative place on my writing journey, to the more technical side of what makes a story tick.

I suggest you start by visiting www.storygrid.com and getting all the free resources, explore the blog, listen to the podcast. And after you've spent some time doing that, should you decide it's something you want to try, there is a Story Grid book you can purchase to take you step-by-step through the Story Grid Method. Sean Coyne is an editor and a publisher, and he knows what he's talking about. He was finding it hard to work for the big publishing houses because he didn't feel that there was a really good process in place to determine which books worked and which didn't. So, he stepped away from those companies and created his own editing business around the Story Grid.

Five minutes listening to him speak on the subject, and you will see he's not only extremely intelligent—not just about story, but in general—but he has such a big heart, and a deep passion for helping writers make their stories work. This is the real reason I became obsessed with his work. I felt his passion behind his knowledge, and after I used the Story Grid Method for my last novel, I was convinced he was my go to guide to revise my first draft and evolve it into a presentable piece of work to send to an editor.

That is the purpose of the Story Grid, to get your book ready for an editor. Or, if you choose to edit yourself, to complete a thorough edit of your work.

So what's next? Look into the Story Grid. Begin revising your draft. If the Story Grid doesn't resonate with you, some other great resources are Jeff Goins, Stephen King's book, *On Writing*, the Neil Gaiman's Masterclass. **But this is essential: never give their opinions more power than your own intuition when deciding how to revise your book, no matter how successful they are. Only you know what is right for your book. Take what you want and leave the rest.**

Even though we're now stepping out a little from the *inner writer's journey*, that doesn't mean it's time to hand your power as an author over to anyone else. These are simply suggestions to give you guidance in the revision process. If you want to revise using your own methods, and you feel confident you're being guided along that path, then do so!

The purpose of living the *internal writer's journey* is to write your book without anything outside of yourself, or YOU, getting in the way. It's the path to opening yourself up to the creative forces of the Universe to work through you, and with you, to write your book. If you can get to this place, and write your entire book in this way, then by the time you're ready to revise, edit, and publish—which are the times you will want to seek out someone who knows what to do—you're in a place of peace and confidence to know what feels right and what doesn't. No one can tell you what's right for your book. Only you get to decide that.

Ending Payoff

�֎

Rising Into the Light

You Are
An Author

My intention with this book was to invite you into a new way of seeing your writing journey. I remember how alone and fearful I felt when I began all those years ago, and I wish I had someone who would have told me everything I've shared in this book because it would have saved me so much inner turmoil. The writing journey can be lonely enough without fear and doubt floating around in your head or your heart.

I have faith that, if you've gotten this far, you've made the shift from floating in the darkness to rising into the light. If you have a finished draft in your hands by this point, then I know you have made that shift. You don't have to do it alone, nor are you.

Instead of seeking someone else in this physical world to tell you how to write a book, or what to write, turn inward and find the answers from the Divine Source of the Universe. It lives within you. It always has, only your ego was too much in the way for you to feel it. Set your ego aside, step out of the way, and let yourself be guided as a writer. After all, it was this Divine Source that instilled your passion to be writer within you because it had big dreams for you to make great change through your stories in this lifetime.

You let go of your ego and step out of the way by getting quiet through mediation. I can't emphasize this enough. Meditation is your key to unlocking the *internal writer's journey*. There is no other way. Start with five minutes a day if that's as long as you can sit still. You want to get to a place where twenty to forty minutes each day is normal for you. But for now, just do as much as you can and slowly grow into it.

You will find after a time that you yearn for your meditation time. It's the moments where you will feel most connected to your source and to your creativity. I meditate for twenty minutes, two time a day. This time is precious to me, and if I don't get it now, I find myself spinning my wheels and I get unproductive both in writing and in life. Start with an app like Insight Timer. Find meditations that make you feel good, that allow you to quiet your mind, and get connected to that higher power within you.

I personally love the meditations from Wayne Dyer: *I Am Wishes Fulfilled Meditation* and *Meditations for Manifesting*. Which meditations you use doesn't matter. You don't have to use any, but to sit in quiet for twenty minutes and go within. That's where the magic happens—where your ideas for your books will come, where guidance on the next steps after writing the book will come, and much more.

You are an author. This is only the beginning of an exciting writing journey for you. I can't wait for you to discover what that is for you.

Keep dreaming, always write your story, and most importantly—believe in the power you hold within to create anything you want.

Join The Community

Thank you for embarking on this journey. I intend that you've experienced the shift from the *external writer's journey* to the *internal writer's journey*, and that you are beginning to feel within yourself all the power you hold as a writer. Everything you need to write your novel exists inside of you. Go within and believe in your Higher Self to guide you toward anything you may need to write your novel.

If you would like to learn more, I'd love to have you in the community! You can join by signing up for the email list, listening to the podcast, reading my novels, or applying to work with me on your novel. I'm excited to connect with you! Sending love and gratitude,

Alysia Seymour
www.alysiaseymour.com

About the Author

Alysia Seymour is a fantasy author who loves to explore stories through a spiritual and internal focused lens. She believes fantasy stories are the gateway to our imaginations, not only within fantasy worlds, but within our own lives. Through her novels, Alysia uses her own life experiences as her story ideas and to create real, vulnerable characters.

After writing three novels in this way, and coaching her clients to do the same, Alysia decided to write a book on the subject of the internal writer's journey to make this idea more accessible to aspiring fiction writers.

She writes in a straightforward, honest, and unveiling way that allows the readers to absorb the ideas presented in a way that's personal to them. Through this book, Alysia guides you to a new perspective on what it means to be a fiction author, exposing the side of the writing journey that isn't as popular to talk about—the internal journey.